Poet of the

musings of a global peacemaker

By "Mama Lizzie"

Published by Candala Publishing

ISBN 978-0-9571398-0-0

www.mamalizzie.com

"At a touch of love, everyone becomes a poet"

Plato

Mama Lizzie

Lizzie Davies, affectionately known as "Mama Lizzie" is an innovator, artist, writer and performance poet actively involved in the creation and promotion of peace. She wrote and performed her own one-woman show Performance Piece, has recited her work on BBC Radio and at a wide range of events such as peace conferences in the UK and also abroad.

She is Founder of The Global Circle of Peace[1] and founded Time for Peace - an interactive arts project which was a recipient of the 1999 Gordon Wilson Peace Award given by The Week of Prayer for World Peace.

Lizzie is the originator of the CANDALA®[2] and Creative Director of the CANDALA® Project. Trained at the Adam Darius School of Mime in Hampstead, London she has over thirty years experience in the arts and personal development and is an experienced presenter, workshop facilitator and event organiser.

She is passionate about sharing her path of creative expression and self-transformation which is based on a holistic perspective, a synthesis of spiritual and psychological understanding and her life experience which includes being a cult-survivor.

[1] www.theglobalcircleofpeace.com.
[2] A CANDALA® is an illuminated art form to light up our world. Full definition and Guidelines can be found at www.theglobalcircleofpeace.com/get-involved/.

Dedicated to

My parents, Marie Blanche Davies and David Harold Davies

Eric Lomax

and

"our children and our children's children"

Acknowledgements

I would like to acknowledge all the people who have helped me on my journey of discovery, especially those who have shared my vision and contributed to my peace work over the years.

I also wish to thank most warmly everyone who has made this book possible: Alan and Sosi, Adam Fotheringham, Margaret Gibney, the Browne Family, Marc Erdrich, Rhonda King, Hardy Jones, management and the staff at the Buccament Bay Resort, notably, Mark Sawkins, Matt Baker, Candida Depleche, Francisca D. Clarke, David N. Samuel, Gennine Da Breo and Desrick Gordon.

Production Team

Susan Rowe, Editor

Photography: Caroline Dewison, Dick Foster - TriMedia Enterprises

and Peter J. Stone

Layout: Sean Fretwell

Be Original – Be Yourself

My personal motto is Be Original – Be Yourself. It encapsulates all that I hold most dear, for as I see it, to be original is to be an instrument of God and the prime injunction is to know yourself. I am profoundly committed to this path of self-realisation, which, in essence, I have found to be the practice of deep faith, unconditional love and service to your community. I do my very best to learn, give and receive this teaching every day in whatever way I can and to be grateful for whatever the day brings.

For those of you who may not share my spiritual view, you may still perhaps acknowledge the existence of some kind of higher power, whatever name you choose to call it.

The Vincy Muse and "Mama Lizzie"

On the second day of my return visit to St. Vincent and the Grenadines, in October this year, a *Vincy Muse* whispered in my ear "Poet of the Caribbean." This prompted a poem of the same name, more poetry and the idea of a small book. In addition, after two weeks, I had been given the name *"Mama Lizzie"* by a Vincentian woman young enough to be my daughter. Even this seemed to be a natural and timely fit – not just for personal reasons, but because all of my work is dedicated to:

'our children and our children's children'

As I pondered on how to frame the work of 'Poet of the Caribbean' and what original angle the book might convey, it became clear that it was to serve the *Bigger Picture* and was to be a vehicle to tell my story. The latter came as a bombshell. Initially, I felt shocked and resistant. Still, I have learnt to trust my intuition and the ways of the creative spirit...

As the process unfolded, everything began to piece itself together. The strap-line musings of a global peacemaker was to reflect a whole range of perspectives on peacemaking and also promote The Global Circle of Peace – a new way of uniting the people of the world through a creative movement for universal peace.

World Peace is a topic that is often immediately discarded as impossible to achieve. This is largely because it is not seen as having any direct relationship to our own state of mind and being. We are all inter-connected. How we think, what we say and the words we choose to use to express ourselves, shape our reality and that of others at any given moment.

Darkness and light, war and peace go hand in hand. In sharing my musings and my story, may this book stimulate reflection, conversation, healing, transformation and understanding. My intention is that in being so open and honest, this will inspire, empower and uplift other people and perhaps allow you to see something in a new light.

My Story

Creativity has been my salvation. I first came to St. Vincent in May 2011 at the end of an intensive six month course of treatment for PTSD (Post Traumatic Stress Disorder) which had severely crippled my life for nearly eighteen years. The symptoms were such that they rendered me dysfunctional in the outside world for more than six months every year with all the complexities that this engendered, as I could also function at an extremely high level when I was well. Indeed, I was crystal clear that I had embarked on a last-ditch attempt at getting the help I needed to overcome my condition as my life had become unbearable the way it was. It was simple. If the treatment didn't work, I was out of here and had made my peace with that decision.

Whilst at this crossroads, I was given the means to devote myself to an in-depth course of treatment which I tailor-made to my needs. The holistic interventions included cutting-edge brain treatment, psychological counselling using the imagination, homeopathy, breathwork and bodywork. As always creativity came to my rescue and I found a new powerful way of working with the synthesized use of symbols, archetypes, artwork and rhyming poetry.

The work was lonely and gruelling and one of the deepest tests of my faith, endurance and courage. Nevertheless, I was in the best possible hands, trusted my guides and was determined to give it my all. The work paid off and I rewarded myself with a two week holiday in the Caribbean staying at the five star Buccament Bay Resort in St. Vincent and the Grenadines. My stay was quite magical and I immediately fell in love with the local people and the land. I returned home a new woman ready to begin a whole new life and make up for lost time.

I had a clear, intuitive lead for the immediate next phase of my life as I knew the spirit had called me back to St. Vincent for a reason that I had yet to discover. Indeed, this prompting was so strong that I spent the next four months putting my house in order and making practical plans to accommodate this major leap of faith. Just before I left, I bought myself a signet ring inscribed with the words of Plato[3].

[3]Refer to opening quote.

It is possible, with hindsight, to see almost anything as a blessing in disguise. Had I not endured extreme loss, abuse, mental illness and several breakdowns (known as breakthroughs nowadays!) in different periods of my life, I would never have done the deep psychological, spiritual and healing work of self-transformation that was needed to fulfil my destiny.

As a cult-survivor late in life, my experience of spiritual, mental, emotional and financial abuse was one of total annihilation. Losing my beloved new husband, my home, all my money and possessions and nearly my mind, was all part of my *trial by fire*. To put this in context, I had been a wealthy woman and now had approximately £40 to my name. My parents had passed on, my brother had turned his back on me and there were no other family members to whom I could turn. I was, however, blessed by the extraordinary generosity of a virtual stranger who took me in and offered to house and feed me for three months.

My spiritual life and first-hand experience of mind-control, undue influence and desire to fathom the depths of psychological programming and peer-pressure could only mean one thing, dedicating the rest of my life to the creation of peace and reconciliation in the world, using the arts as a medium of bridge-building.

When I left the cult in 1993, two significant things happened. Firstly, in response to hearing the news, my dear friend, Walter Speight in America, wrote me a letter in which he enclosed the following quotation:

> *"He drew a circle that shut me out Heretic, rebel, a thing to flout. But love and I had the wit to win, We drew a circle and took him in."*
>
> *from the poem "Outwitted" THE SHOES OF HAPPINESS and other poems, Edwin Markham (1915)*

These words arrived as if in answer to my prayers and provided me with inspired guidance that I could refer to again and again on the long road of forgiveness and recovery that I knew lay ahead. The rhyme of the verse enabled the words to become a regular mantra *and a friend*. In addition, I had the symbol of *the*

Circle to play with which became a catalyst and yardstick for measuring my own progress.

So deeply did *the Circle* become etched in my being that this led to the creation of the CANDALA®4 which is based on *the Circle* and the founding of The Global Circle of Peace.

Secondly, in those very early days a number of people said that I would one day work on the world stage. I knew in my soul that this was true, yet such was my wounding and my 'shell-shock', that I was not sure if I would ever fully recover and become victor over my circumstance.

It has taken eighteen years of dedicated inner and outer work coupled with the help of wonderful friends and professionals to integrate and become a well-rounded human being. Now in the autumn of my years, I am at peace and thank God for all that has happened in my life. It is time to pass on the teaching that I have been given to others and to stand simply and nakedly where life has trained me to be.

St. Vincent and the Grenadines
October 2011

4See image page

In Mama Lizzle's Words

HEARTBEAT

The Voice of I AM
The Call

MY CURRICULUM VITAE

Sexy Hymn – celebrating woman

MY TESTIMONY

The Art of Creativity

DYING TO BE BORN

Reclaiming My Self
The Possible Vision
My Blossoming Tree
A Way Through
Revelation
The Unsung Sound
Companion to the Fallen
No Kin! No Kin!
Hush My Broken Child
Solid as a Rock – my warrior song
The Long Walk
Reaching for the Stars
Wire Me Up For Loving
Dear Mr. Lomax

HEARTBEAT

In May 1995, I was on a week's retreat house-sitting for friends in the country, just outside Bath, UK, when I experienced an extraordinary phenomenon. I was taking a shower when all of a sudden I heard and felt the heartbeat of Mother Earth. It moved through me in a flash and I can only describe it as having been played by a loud, deep, throbbing pulse which sounded and felt like a big base drum. Despite having no reference of understanding for such an experience, I had a sense of knowing what it was.

I was accustomed to having unusual things happen to me in terms of receiving inspirational guidance and decided to reflect on what had occurred. I was already taking time out away from the world to contemplate and listen to the quiet, small voice within, so it seemed the perfect timing for inner enquiry. The whole experience had moved me profoundly and caused me to question how I could use this heightened state of awareness and "message" from Mother Earth to be her mouthpiece.

That week marked the 50th anniversary of the ending of the 2nd World War and the imminent 50th anniversaries of the two atomic bombings against the cities of Hiroshima and Nagasaki in Japan. The television coverage was full of deeply disturbing imagery and commentary. It was impossible to comprehend the related death and suffering through the statistics and the horrific images presented. All I could do was to bear witness.

By the end of the week I had written two poems - *Heartbeat* and *the Call*. I share here just four lines from the poem *Heartbeat* which I have entitled *The Voice of I AM* as this seems to be the nub of the message that could, if practiced, cause humanity to become more balanced and sane.

The Masculine Principal and male-dominant thinking overrides so many cultures and parts of our society, especially in the West, leaving *The Feminine Principal* with its receptive, listening and compassionate nature way behind. When cut off from our body, our spiritual roots and our connection to the earth, we can become lofty, ego-inflated and dangerous. We would do well to stop vaunting our intellectual knowledge and parading our list of achievements to rebalance our focus by exercising the organ of the heart.

The Voice of I AM

To the man in woman,
And the woman in man
I implore you to find
The voice of I AM.

The Call[5]

The mind of man has gone mad - It is sad,
We've forgotten who we are, strayed far,
We are one tribe, remember?
The Truth is inscribed in you and me,
And the whole of humanity,
In communion, we're three in one.
We need to take heed
Of the dangers of vested indoctrination -
The patriarchal planting of the fearful seed;
Love cannot be acquired
Through spiritual or material greed,
Or sold for gold through *enlightened* merchandise;
Light is given and received through the eyes,
Wisdom is woven through the willingness of the wise -
This is The Way of Woman.
To ask and pray,
To honour, listen and obey -
To show, not shout,
To leave no tiny stone unturned;
Cast no lesser person out,
To be kind, not scorn the ordinary
Or belittle the simple mind.
To be mad, glad and sad,
And not pretend...
To know in life there is no beginning and no end...
To sit on the ground and feel the sound -
Of the heartbeat that unites us all,
This, to me, is *The Call*...
The voice of the great Earth Mother.

[5]Written for the spoken word.

MY CURRICULUM VITAE

Finding one's voice for anyone who has been abused, oppressed or traumatised is an extremely significant milestone on their road to recovery. We all lead lives where the intake of information, the people we socialise with and the language we use is influenced or controlled in some way by our environment, culture and peer groups. However, when someone has an ulterior motive to gain dominion over you, it is all part of a plan to increase their power over your mind, behaviour and all aspects of your inner and outer life. Their aim is to silence you, to interfere with your mind and/or body, to break your spirit so that you become a puppet who can be manipulated for their own selfish, greedy and sick ends. Buying your silence through terrorising you is a part of their sinister 'game' and perpetuates the vicious cycle of entrapment.

To access and heal deep trauma is a very complex and lengthy process as often the wounding cannot be verbalised. It was quite a few years before I realised that my love of silence, it's quiet, calm, soothing balm and the access it gave me to inspiration, creativity and serenity was only half the story. I had been silenced and a part of me had become mute. Exploring the underbelly of that silence and giving it sufficient space to surface took a very long time indeed.

I was determined from the very start of my healing journey to be very honest with myself and not go the route of denial. Having been through *Jungian6 analysis* over thirty years ago, I am very mindful of my own shadow and reasoned that it was better not to forgive honestly, to own my darker nature and embrace my human frailty than 'to forgive' and not know that I was harbouring unconscious murderous thoughts and feelings.

For me personally, creativity was one of the keys in my becoming free and it was through working intensively with counsellor and former nun, Jean Roberts, over a period of a year, that I came to originate the art form of the CANDALA®.

6Carl Gustav Jung (26 July 1875 – 6 June 1961) Swiss psychologist Founder of Analytic Psychology.

Transmuting vengeance is a full-time job! During this period, I used to work out at the gym regularly and took up boxing that was extremely therapeutic and a very practical outlet for my rage. One day I was walking across Victoria Park in Bath on the way to the gym, when I became aware of just how much better I was feeling. There was a bounce in my step, a smile on my face and my body felt upright, strong and connected. As I listened more deeply to my body, the rhythm of *Sexy Hymn* came to me and the words of the first verse soon followed.

It may seem a strange thing to some to self-disclose in this manner but I am happy to do it for two reasons. Firstly, because the *dark night of the soul* is a universal journey with which people will resonate and secondly because I wanted to be transparent about who and what was behind The Global Circle of Peace. Having been 'caught' myself by the smokescreens and mirrors of an altruistic sounding spiritual leader with supposed, humanitarian values. I thought at least this way, people will know who and what they are getting and will be able to make up their own mind whether they feel I have something valuable to offer them or not.

We live in a world where the 'Divided Mind' is evident in all kinds of ways: darkness-light, left-brain/right-brain, body-mind, spiritual-material, being-doing, heaven-earth rich-poor and our little and great selves. My life has been full of extremes, which has taught me the importance of bridging polarities.

The original version of *Sexy Hymn* marked the finale of my one-woman show. I added a whole new section in 2010 and performed the updated version at a women's gathering in Stroud Gloucestershire to celebrate International Women's Day (IWD) on 8th March.

It was a dear friend, the original supporter of The Global Circle of Peace, Abdullah Ali-Ahmadi, who observed "Lizzie, *Sexy Hymn* is your Curriculum Vitae!"

Sexy Hymn[7]

I'm a real, real woman
With my own authentic voice,
I've lived and died and risen
And have faced the final choice,
I'm empty and full of paradox -
A walking mystery,
I'm a woman who's discovered
The joy of being me...

I've lived on the edge
And visited the void -
That space which we fear,
And try so hard to avoid,
But in surrendering so completely
To *the dark night of the soul,*
I was moved beyond my little self -
Found oneness with the whole.

I've been through very lean times,
Had habits of excess -
Now I know unconditional love
Is the real meaning of success -
I've fought for survival,
I've climbed up the wall,
I've danced with my demons,
And made peace with them all...

I don't call myself religious
Cos dogmas aren't my scene,
But a life well-lived that is spiritual
Is a thing on which I'm keen -
If we are to be an instrument
Of the one whom I call God,
One thing we surely need to forge
Is a strong divining rod...

7Celebrating woman.

A dog collar's not my uniform
Cos I'm not a thorough breed -
But I love The Lord, who called me,
And from Him I take my lead;
I'm not afraid to be imperfect
Or to stumble *au contraire*,
When I draw from the universe
The canvas must be bare.

It is sobering and challenging
To find the will to dare,
And aspire to lead a life
That is a testament to prayer,
But we need to build a culture
Of spirit without bars -
Of bodies that are vessels
Open to the stars.

The pursuit of self-knowledge,
Is man's eternal quest
An in the moment choice,
To discern the very best;
Every day is an adventure -
Who will we become?
More than we ever dreamt of -
Or stay stuck, asleep and numb?

It often takes a wake-up call -
A test or trial by fire,
To give us the opportunity
To rebuild our life entire;
Like beads upon a necklace
And jewels on a string -
The diamonds of our deepest trials,
Are gems of suffering...

I've been tried, I've been tested,
I've ranted and I've railed,
I've been humiliated -
I've spectacularly failed,
It used to depress me,
It worried me to death;
Until I discovered the wisdom
In each and every breath.

When I looked at myself
In the mirror on the wall,
I was moved by deep compassion
And embraced my human fall,
As I died to old attachments
I was born again and again,
Grace and inspiration
Transmuting all my pain...

I offered up my heavy heart -
A large and weighty gift,
Would it be too burdensome
For the powers that be to lift?
I wonder what the angels said
On pondering the pile,
"O my God! It's her again,
Just humour her and smile!"

I'm an earthy, earthy woman
Rooted like a tree;
My leaves are vibrating
With this living poetry,
It feels like a fusion
Of body, soul and mind;
With a muse who is playful
And with whom I am aligned.

Sex and spirituality
There's really no divide,
When love is moving through us
There is nowhere we can hide;
I'm the actress and the bishop,
I'm the master and the nun,
I'm the bride and the virgin
On fire with faith and fun.

I'm a hoot and I'm haughty,
I am humble and I'm high,
I am good and I am naughty,
I am mighty and I'm shy;
Sometimes I'm zany
And don't care what people think -
Other times I'm bashful
And easily turn pink!

I can be superficial
Or seriously profound -
Or a, high high, flyer
Who's enchanted and spellbound;
I can be very generous
On occasions I've been mean,
I can be bored to distraction -
Or sharp, astute and keen.

I can be hot - I can be cold,
I've dealt someone a blow,
Sometimes I am horrible -
So what? At least I know!
I'm very complicated
And simple in my taste,
I like the best of everything,
With very little waste.

I'm a multi-petalled being,
A soft and velvet flower,
A most unusual specimen -
Who's growing by the hour;
Now I've come into the open,
For everyone to see;
I no longer have to be afraid -
No-one can step on me.

I refuse to be downtrodden,
I refuse to be cut down,
I refuse to hide myself
Behind a false society gown,
I'm enjoying this exposure,
I'm lapping up the light,
I'm loving this attention -
My spirit's taking flight.

It's time to sing my praises -
It's time to sing my song,
Rejoice in all my glory,
Feeling right instead of wrong -
I don't know where it's leading
But I've got a kind of hunch -
That something's quietly cooking
And I know it isn't lunch!

I've always been in conflict,
But now, I am at peace -
United in my inner world
Helps outer wars to cease;
I'm on a real woman catwalk -
A new fashion to impart,
Emblazoned across my bosom
Is the Fire of the Heart!

Now I'm feeling all electric
The air is turning blue,
The current's been switched on -
Inside of me - inside of you?
I'm plugged into the universe,
A bright and lively wire -
I'm going to set the world alight
My soul has caught on fire!

Spring's around the corner -
There is magic in the air,
I'm naturally blossoming -
I'm plump with love and prayer;
I'm putting out my mating call -
I'm sending out the vibe,
I've called up the angels -
I've written to the scribe.

So now I'm looking at the calendar
I'm crossing off the days,
I'm plumping up the pillows
Garnet roses fill my gaze;
Sock me with the jasmine -
Throw me grapes from the vine,
Be lavish with the olive oil -
Be generous with the wine.

Be feminine, be masculine,
Be all that you can be -
Celebrate your sacred self -
Embody unity...
Now I've found my inner woman
And I've found my inner man -
I'm a faithful loving mistress
To the grand old master plan.

Nothing now can stop me,
I'm rocking on a roll
I'm heading for the jackpot
To satisfy my soul!

MY TESTIMONY

Creativity has been my saving grace and is what I know most about. *The Art of Creativity* was driven by my desire to document the multi-dimensional levels of understanding that I have gleaned through my studies and practice of the interconnection between body-mind-spirit and my own experience of creativity.

Not knowing if it would ever be published, I reasoned that at least I had documented my knowledge of creativity in a very succinct and original way that could perhaps be useful to someone one day even if it were after I was gone.

The Art of Creativity

The art of creativity is our innate ability
To express at any one time;
Our highest aspiration and deepest truth
A cross 'twixt the human and sublime,
Ever-present in us all, is a power we can call upon
Whenever we are yearning to be free -
By embodying inspiration, we can access liberation
Through *the Source* – Creativity.

The creative spirit is ingenious,
In a flash, things can change for evermore -
A spark might strike in the dead of night
Or when we don't focus on the problem anymore;
Something can click through spontaneous laughter
Lateral thinking or innocent play -
The flames often take, when the heat is beneath our feet -
When we get ourselves out of the way.

The power to enthuse is oft bestowed by the Muse
When we are aligned to a stillness of mind,
When we're anchored and centred in our bodies -
A quiet place is cleared for us to find;
Beyond the 'little' me, lies our true identity -
The seed of the great I AM...
Which loves to manifest, when we stop to take a rest -
From the crazy busy business log-jam.

The art of creativity is sacred unity -
Borne of the male and female within;
Through the marriage of our innermost *Love-Wisdom*,
We deepen our connection to our kin;
If we want to build a sense of community
And find meaning in a real place,
We must counter our obsession with the outer
Through the exploration of inner space.

Cultivating stillness is a contemplative art -
Engendering the culture of *the Whole* of which we're part;
In listening to ourselves, we get in touch with who we are,
The lost aspects of our nature are collected from afar,
In slowing down our pace, we're more willing to embrace
The unknown and put ourselves to one side;
Which signals the move to get into the groove
Of our intuition - our teacher and guide.

Silence is to sound - what space is to form -
When we gain our perfect poise
We can move beyond the norm;
Accessing dimensions hidden to our outer eye and ear,
Through lighting up our consciousness
A new world can appear -
Miracles happen, synchronicities abound
As we refine our awareness of the vibration of sound.

The art of creativity is pure receptivity,
Through the bridge of our body-mind -
We are attuned to become living instruments -
Contributing our gifts to humankind;
To access our inner voice, is an in the moment choice -
A daily practice through our presence of mind;
To be, or not to be? To see, or not to see?
To do, or not to do? Pretend we're blind?

Why did we break *the Circle*?
Life doesn't live in straight lines,
Through cutting our bond with Nature
We've stopped seeing the Wonders and Signs;
Whatever the manifold reasons
Now, is the time to reconnect,
To Life in all of its seasons
        Humanity is ours to resurrect.

Creativity follows *the Circle of Life*
According to Universal law,
In our cycles, rhythms and patterns
Lies the key to our sacred door -
Through circulating energy
Time and time again,
There's always the chance to step into the dance
        Whatever our past or our pain...

The art of creativity is the focus of acuity -
A lazar that can cut to the core,
Insight with rigour and mindfulness
And a compassionate intent to restore;
Can enable the light of discernment,
To lift the veil from our eyes -
So we find the courage to live our truth
        And sever our negative ties.

The ultimate experiment is ours to manifest,
If we face our greatest demons and take on board the test -
We have to die to be reborn, all the time in little ways
So the patterns of the past are not repeated all our days;
If our spirit is to fly, we must pass through gates of death
Rising as the Phoenix - with each and every breath;
By surrendering our little selves on to the sacred pyre,
        Our soul is reignited by the one creative fire.

The art of creativity is the essence of simplicity,
Conveyed with authenticity and skill -
Whatever our medium and message
We all have a role to fulfil;
If we're to move beyond our safe limitations
And redeem who we truly are,
We need to trust ourselves and each other
    And be determined to follow our star.

We all have infinite potential -
Our brain's lying half asleep,
Imagine if everyone here and now
Made a promise to dig down deep -
And every day on awakening
Chose not to stay the same -
But to realise their unique potential,
    Which bears their very own name.

The art of creativity is heightened sensitivity
Connection to our purpose and our power -
When our energy has dwindled
We can choose to be rekindled -
Life is the Tao[8] of the now;
Dare to open the door, let your inner fire roar,
Let your passion like a beacon burn bright...
May your imagination light up our constellation
    Blaze a trail across the indigo night!

[8]Chinese word meaning 'way' or 'path'.

DYING TO BE BORN

Poem I

It was during the first week of my 'freedom' having left the cult, that I wrote *Reclaiming My Self*. The first verse, in particular, became an important mantra that I used to repeat as I went about my daily business. I knew that I had to fight for survival at all levels of my being and it gave me enormous strength and fuelled my fighting spirit. The last two verses are in a sense prophetic and can be seen to refer to now and the publication of this book.

Poems II-VII

The next six poems were written in a tiny room in London the size of a prison cell. I lived there for a year and realised that if I were to survive I must envision my future and believe that I could manifest a positive, new life. Given the fact that I was still shell-shocked having lost virtually everything that constituted my life, it was tremendously challenging to hold the possibility of building anything afresh. The power and practice of creative visualisation at this critical time was my life-line.

Poems VIII-IX

I wrote *No Kin! No Kin!* and *Hush My Broken Child* on retreat whilst house sitting for friends. These poems marked a turning point in my healing journey and from that point on I started to write daily and express myself visually for the first time since I was a teenager. Both of these things were a great help in focusing my mind, a much needed skill, as I was fighting a major legal battle against the cult for 'undue influence' which, at the time, was a rare case. It was particularly distressing as the organisation, a registered charity, had put my now former husband in charge of the litigation against me.

Poem X

Solid as a Rock is my warrior song. In December 1995, I was so wearied by my mental, emotional, spiritual and legal struggle that I lost my nerve and felt I couldn't go through with it all. I felt broken and suicidal and was daunted not only by the potentially high-profile trial, with media interest, but having to face a raft of people who had been my 'family' and were now testifying against me, including my former husband. An inspired friend gave me a gift of a large heart-shaped stone which prompted the idea and theme of the poem and my friend, singer-songwriter Shirlie Roden, set *Solid as a Rock* to music. Singing the song with friends and on my own helped me find the courage to stand firm. The organisation made an out-of-court settlement just before going to the High Court of Justice in London.

Poem XI

I have left *the Long Walk* largely unedited as I feel it reflects very accurately the state of mind that I was in at the time and offers a window of understanding into the effect of major loss and the perennial dilemma of the 'agony and ecstasy' polarities that face those who have sensitivities beyond the 'normal' range of perception. I also hope that it might help to shed light on the collective responsibility that society has to recognise the existence of bona-fide spiritual gifts and to nurture and support those who need informed guidance and education on how to develop their awareness in a safe, reliable way.

Most importantly, it is vital that those who offer such training do not have a vested interest in abusing the gifts of their students for their own ends. In my view, a solid psychological grounding is especially important when navigating the more subtle spiritual realms. It is here that delusion, denial and the heady use of power over other people can be rife. Humility, discernment, self-reflection and the willingness to be questioned and held accountable for one's actions are a healthy antidote to such ego mania.

I wrote *the Long Walk* in 2001 during a two week stay at Wellspring Retreat and Resource Centre in Albany, Ohio USA. The Centre treats people who have been victims of psychological, emotional or spiritual abuse from religious cults, toxic relationships or other manipulative groups. I was privileged to work 1-1 with the late Dr. Paul Martin, a psychologist and founder of Wellspring, himself a cult-survivor. He was very moved by my story and it made all the difference to me that one person, who understood, and had been *there* himself, had born witness to what I had been through. I never imaged that this poem would ever see the light of day or be shared with even one other person apart from Paul. I have come to see, however, that it is important to 'tell it as it is' or in this case 'was' and not to cover up the stigma of mental illness or the ignorance and judgement that is projected on those who suffer in this way.

Poems XII & XIII

The last two poems, *Reaching for the Stars* and *Wire Me Up for Loving* are examples of what I call my *Word Remedies* for encapsulating the essence of a particular idea. In this case, I was experimenting with creative visualisation. Envisioning a positive future and a healthy functioning mind and brain, I used to recite these *Word Remedies* frequently throughout the day so that they became like a self-hypnosis programme. Words were my medicine and I thought of them as my building blocks to a positive new life.

Reclaiming My Self

You cannot beat me
You will not win,
        For the wind of God is behind me
        And the power of truth within.

You cannot hurt me
You cannot cause me pain,
        I've gone beyond your distorted mind
        To where *Life* can be born in me again.

You cannot own me
You cannot have my soul,
        This is my dominion
        Outside your reach and control.

You cannot break me
However hard you try,
        My spirit will fight even stronger
        For every single tear that I cry.

Your cruelty cannot touch me
Your brutal words are a shell,
        I've withstood the trials of the tortured
        And made steel out of living through hell...

The love you wield is a weapon
In a glove of invisible deceit,
        All you've ever made in your blindness
        Will one day lie stark at your feet.

What can't you take away from me?
All that is inside,
>
> My courage and my dignity
> The parts that almost died...

What can't you extinguish?
The will that wants to go on,
>
> The flame that fires my furnace
> The spirit that kindles my song...

I know not how justice will happen
Nor do I need to know,
>
> For it is God who will one day deliver
> My duty in this is to grow.

God propel me forward
Help me make the moves I need,
>
> Help me carry the cross of bereavement
> And plant peace in the form of a seed.

There is a bigger picture
That one day will unfold,
>
> When the threads all come together
> My story will be told.

I will wait for the hour to be given
For each piece to be put in its place,
>
> Then when I feel all the wheels turn as one
> I will trust in myself and God's Grace.

The Possible Vision

Can I use all this death and destruction
To live and build something new?
Can I promise to leave and totally believe
In the possible vision of a beautiful view?

My Blossoming Tree

There will be a blossom on my tree,
This winter waste will fade -
I will one day stand again
Rooted and triumphant, swaying and serene,
The wind of Life blowing through me
The pain having passed through my veins.

A Way Through

How is there a way through? O Wise One
Will you show me a new view?
A place from where I can sit and see,
Apart from being engulfed by agony?
"Suffering can destroy and imprison
Or sweep the path clear for new life - which is to be?"
Why have you left me bereft of everything?
"To be me..."

Revelation

There's a tender hand that is leading me
Way beyond my sight,
The path is not seen but revealing beneath
In the dark and death of night.

The Unsung Sound

I have yet to cross the Unsung Sound,
I will wait -
Until quiet indwells the dawn,
And in still remembering -
Life will breathe me.

Companion to the Fallen

What is the call to action?
Where is the map to be found?
For learning how to love your enemy,
       In a way that is honest and sound?

Looking in the mirror
Reflecting quiet within,
I have glimpsed the lure of entrapment
       In the face of *others'* sin.

So I must be my own companion
Staying still by my side,
Not laughing at my folly
       Nor pointing at my pride.

No Kin! No Kin!

The pain of no kin, no kin –
The veil between the worlds so thin;
All the goodbyes are pleated, folded and filed
I do not mind if I stay or go –
But I cannot bear not to use what I know.

Hush My Broken Child

Hush my broken child
The tenderest hand will mend you;
If only you will allow - Lay all of yourself open to rest,
And quietly lie down with me now.

Let me wrap you in my raiment
Anoint you with my balm,
Cradle you deep in my lullaby
And hold you safe in my arms.

Give the gulf of your grief as a gift to me
Let your tears and terror be wrought,
Endow me with your patience complete
Prepare your pain to pour forth.

Be still and breathe within the breath of me
Belly to belly, mind to mind, heart to heart,
As the mighty flood moves through you
May the bathing of the bile now start.

Weep and wail and wake the wound
Unleash your imprisoned lament,
Gouge and thrash and lash your fury -
Beat on my breast till your hammering is spent.

I will not leave you bereft of me
For where you have died - I will live,
And now you know when you call - I am come
And where there is need - I will give.

SOLID AS A ROCK

SOLID AS A ROCK
ROOTED AS A TREE,
CLEAR AS A CRYSTAL,
SPIRIT STRONG AND FREE.

FIRE IN MY BELLY
PASSION IN MY HEART,
LIGHT IN MY MIND
SHINING BRIGHT FROM THE START.

UPRIGHT FEARLESS
PROTECTION ALL AROUND,
HEAD IN THE HEAVENS
FEET ON THE GROUND.

JUSTICE BALANCE
HARMONY GRACE,
SILENCE PRESENCE
COMPOSED IN ONE PLACE.

LIGHT AS A FEATHER
FLUID AS A STREAM,
STRAIGHT AS AN ARROW
PIERCING THROUGH DREAM.

SWORD OF THE WARRIOR
COURAGE OF THE LION,
PERCEPTION OF THE UNICORN
BACKBONE OF IRON.

POWER OF THE UNIVERSE
LINKING OF THE TRIBE,
NEW BORN INTELLIGENCE
WE ARE THE SCRIBE.

The Long Walk

It is not talk that will change the world
Nor where we have been,
But the walk we make,
Having changed our own being
    As a result of what we've seen.

I've lived a life that no-one knows I've lived -
Locked in trauma, I have stayed
In a small part of myself that is very, very vast;
    Way past the world that most people know

Tortured by what seemed like
An endless living death,
Imprisoned in a body-mind cell,
    I've made frequent descents into unimaginable hell.

Now, I wonder, is it time to show what I have seen
Where I have been wandering –
Alone for so long
    In search of my song.

I am ready to unlock the memories
Come back and face the lack,
Inhabit more the mundane world
    And not fly away because I cannot bear the pain.

The more I melt,
The more I see how much of me has been frozen,
Pinned to the ground - voiceless, choice-less,
    Just going round and round and round.

I've stood on the edge of madness,
Filled with unspeakable loss and sadness,
So punch-drunk with pity and pain,
I just wanted to throw away the key
    And never come back again.

Imprinted in me for ever
Is the day when the clouds parted,
And in a sudden moment of cool clarity
That seemed like an eternity
    I chose to save my own sanity.

I surveyed the scene of being tended in bed for ever
And said 'No'!
I will walk back from the wild-eyed side of life,
And when I do, I will fly the flag
    For the less fortunate and the few.

How many men and women of vision
Have been vilified because
They saw more than they could bear,
Because no-one cared enough to glimpse another land
    Or take time to understand?

How many voices deemed absurd
Were simply muddled streams of consciousness,
Displaced screams of recorded horror
    That went un-coded and remained unheard?

My creativity has sometimes felt like
An affliction - an addiction,
Defence against the mad reality
    People call the "real" world.

What, I wonder, do they see that is real?
From where I am sitting so much in our society is sick
And so blatantly counterfeit,
The majority live *the Lie* and pretend we do not die,
    Is this not madness?

My vision has often felt like a blessing *and* a curse,
My most treasured friend and most faithful nurse,
Yet how terrible is the blame -
The shame and stigma of mental fragility,
Is this the price one has to pay
    For this unbearable sensitivity?

All my life, I have been unable to share or deny
The gifts I have been given,
Dipping at times into deep, resolute acceptance -
And others, crushed by what seemed
    Like an awesome burden of responsibility.

Often I have not wanted to see, hear or feel
What was in my power,
Yet I could not turn my back on a spiritual vow,
Which seemed to be written in my soul -
Love is my life and Truth my ultimate goal.

Thank God for the vast starry space
Of the quiet desert night - its infinite stillness and peace,
Have provided me with sweet balm of solace
And welcome release,
Acute intuition, sublime inspiration, roads of revelation,
Born of acres of time spent in deep contemplation.

Each test in life I have wrestled with
Has brought me closer to an inner serenity and rest,
The God that I have come to know
Is not the one, who is trotted out for show.

Nor the one who shouts what to believe
My God says "Sow your Truth here and now,
All will be seen in what grows behind you when you leave"
By their seeds shall ye know them...

The Power of the Word,
Dark secrets transformed by being heard
Received, believed,
My story no longer just lives in me -

It has taken on its own mystery;
Freely given, no longer driven,
The past can settle and be given its own burial ground,
I can die now, because someone knows how I have lived,
Torment no more, my spirit can soar.

Reaching for the Stars

I am dreaming my life into being
Designing the life I want,
I'm cutting through the bars
Reaching for the stars,
Writing YES in my favourite font!

Wire me up for Loving

If the mind is all a programme
Running circuits through our head,
Wire me up for loving,
Resurrect me from the dead!

Poem XIV

I wrote the poem *Dear Mr. Lomax* in 1995 during one of the most harrowing periods of my life, yet it was also a time that I was at my most creative. Life was a battle and I had barely any social interaction or contact with the outside world. Mentally and emotionally I was still shattered and physically I was at a very low ebb indeed, but my spirit was strong.

I had come to think of rebuilding my mind as a very physical affair. When I looked inside my head, I saw a maze of unwalked corridors and knew that I had to somehow force myself to walk down them to retread some of the old neural pathways of thinking that I had temporarily lost. I knew that I also had to explore new avenues of thought. It was like trying to rewire a house when you are in the dark and know nothing about electricity! The horror of my cult experience at that time was still locked deep inside me. I didn't try to write *Dear Mr. Lomax*, I went to a place I had never visited inside myself and it wrote me...

I first heard about the universal phenomenon of people crying out 'Mother! Mother!' when *in extremis* as I watched a television programme about the 1st World War and the horrors that soldiers endured both in the trenches and on the battlefield. Learning of this piercing heartfelt cry in the face of such terrible suffering had a very profound and lasting effect on me.

The 'Mother! Mother!' call was to play itself out much nearer to home in my own life, albeit by proxy, when I watched a television documentary[9] about Eric Lomax[10] the extraordinarily courageous soldier and inspirational man who was to become my role model on the journey of forgiveness and reconciliation. I happened upon the film, supposedly by chance. Watching it was to change my life.

It was the story of how Mr. Lomax had been tortured by the Japanese on the Burma-Siam Railway and how, fifty years later, he was able to meet one of his Japanese tormentors. Mr. Nagase Takashi, the interrogator who had translated the sadistic orders of his military commander. Nagase was a military interpreter for the Kempeitai, the special Japanese police, in the prison camp made famous in the movie, *Bridge on the River Kwai*, when POW

[9]Enemy My Friend (1995), directed by Mike Finlason.
[10]Eric Lomax, author of the award-winning book '*The Railway Man*'.

Eric Lomax was caught with a concealed radio and map. Lomax was beaten relentlessly and dragged broken and weak before Nagase and his commanding officer for interrogation. Nagase's voice droned in his ear as he was repeatedly held down and water was hosed into his nose and mouth, filling his lungs and stomach. It was during this systematic torture that Lomax cried out 'Mother! Mother!'

The programme re-enacted this terrifying method of water torture used, which was designed to nearly drown its victims by flooding their stomach and lungs. I was struck by the fact that Mr. Lomax had remembered his interrogator's last words to him from all those years ago 'Keep your chin up'. The significance of those few words leapt out at me. It's an expression that conjures up the epitome of *Englishness* in terms of understatement, moral courage and fighting spirit – the kind of backbone of our nation that represents the very best of who we have been and can be. I found it hideously and almost laughably ironic that these were the words uttered by someone who was instrumental in inflicting such relentless brutality. How must it have been for Mr. Lomax to hear those words?

As privileged spectators to the film, we were privy to the meeting between Mr. Lomax and Mr. Takashi on the *Bridge of the River Kwai* and their subsequent conversations which culminated in a simple and profound act of forgiveness, which led to a life-long friendship. We also saw Mrs. Lomax and Mrs. Takashi – the two women who had accompanied their husbands on their private and public journeys to hell and back.

Seeing the film and bearing witness to such deep suffering opened a door for me and I walked through it to discover new depths. I was transfixed by what I had seen and heard. What horrific suffering – mental and physical. Eric Lomax had made the journey of forgiveness that I, in my own relatively small way, wanted one day to make. Here was a living, breathing example – someone of real flesh and blood who had been tortured and dehumanised by the insane and yet somehow found a way to keep his dignity, sanity and humanity. Seeing what Mr. Lomax had been through and transcended made me realise that it was possible to come through what I called 'the Uncomethroughable' and in some strange way, I no longer felt alone.

As I watched Mr. Lomax' story unfold, it penetrated the steel fortress in which I had been incarcerated and I started to weep – for him, for me, and the whole of humanity. I was bowed - both ashamed and inspired by what human beings can do - how low we can sink and how high we can rise...

I sat in a heap on the floor rocking backwards and forwards crying out for help. Gradually, out of the deep, dark, silence, I started to find my voice and the poem moved through me. I found myself speaking out loud repeating the words over and over and over again. What a relief it was to pour my heart out and house my fear and feelings in a safe place outside of myself. I had named the un-namable. In being with Mr. Lomax in his torture and pain it had helped to unlock my own.

Dear Mr. Lomax includes the imagined thoughts and comments of Mr. Takashi which appear in the first four verses in italics.

Dear Mr. Lomax[11]

'It's fifty years on since you struggled,
Not to take your last breath -
We both survived and were sentenced,
To the pain of a long living death;
 I never touched you physically,
 I just tried to break your mind,
 I didn't inflict the torture -
 I'm a civilised man, I am kind.'

'I only watched as they drowned you,
Stood by as you squirmed for your life -
I'm a mild man really, Mr. Lomax
Really ordinary, just ask my wife;
 I was only the interpreter,
 The middle man caught between -
 I was blind and deaf and terrified,
 It's hard to accept where I've been'...

'You were obsessed by the memory,
Of hearing the sound of my voice,
And your eyes kept on haunting me -
That was the price that I paid for my choice;
 Chin up Mr. Lomax -
 Let me look into your eyes,
 Let me see who it is I am loathing,
 And who it is I despise.'

'Destiny brought us together
Life made sure we'd meet
 To learn the lesson the hard way
 To make the bitter taste sweet.'

---

[11] Abridged version.

The Guru, The Tyrant, The Emperor -
The excuse is always the same,
"I did it under orders
It's not me who you have to blame",
    Where is the face of the hangman?
    Who is it that sets the noose?
    Where is the guilty culprit?
    Who holds the key to abuse?

Who then pulls the trigger?
Who then drops the bomb?
Where does responsibility lie?
If not in everyone?
    What about "The Silent One" -
    The one who just looks on
    As party to the secret,
    The lynchpin to the bomb?

It's time to bury the old way,
And the route of the either, the or -
The right or wrong or in or out,
"The Other" we always abhor;
    Evil's a vicious circle,
    Kept in place by the voice
    Of the silenced individuals
    Who dare not speak its name.

Such is the power of corruption,
And the destruction induced through fear,
It can make people cower in its presence
So they totally disappear;
    One day I will cross the barrier,
    And find the way to forgive,
    In the place that now lies barren -
    I am sowing seeds that will live.

I am walking in the shoes of Mr. Lomax,
Daily learning to quiet outstretch my hand
And when I lay the ghost of my tormentors
Only then will I fully understand...
     I want to tell you my story,
     I want to give voice to the void,
     Of the feelings that lie dead and buried
     That for years I've tried to avoid.

Will you listen, Mr. Lomax
To the torture of this child?
Will you share my silent torment
Of the trust that has been fouled and defiled?
     No-one can know my heartbreak -
     No-one can know my pain,
     But I know you know the "Unspoken Place"
     Where words can never reign.

I do not want to burden you,
After all you've had to endure,
     But in reaching out across the way
     My motive is sincere and pure.

There are many pathways to murder,
I know the insidious kind,
Not the dagger dug deep in the body -
But the slow, searing torture of the mind;
    Today I am plagued by the memories,
    Sickened by what I recall,
    But I know in admitting the feelings
    I am dismantling the inner prison wall.

The cell that keeps us captured -
The past that holds us 'there',
The memories only exclude us
From the miracle of Life everywhere;
    I want to release my torment,
    I want to access my pain,
    I am fighting through my writing
    So that Life may come again.

It is vital that I voice it,
And remember the dreaded day,
I want to name the nightmare
To help it go away;
    The rhythm of this poem
    Is the beat upon my breast,
    It conjures up the emotion -
    Makes the wordless manifest.

I'm haunted by the memories
I can hardly bare to see,
I don't know how to exorcise
The hold they have on me;
    No-one knows what happened,
    Nor do they want to know,
    It's as if 'it never happened'
    Which is just another blow.

I watched the people who'd loved me
Become robotic and cold,
The air turned foul and despotic
As fear was made manifold;
  I was now the *enemy, the someone*
  They had to cast out,
  Their unseen shadow projected
  Their only contact with doubt...

I watched them become dismembered,
Witnessed their power run amok,
God's most chosen people,
The elite of 'the Heavenly Flock'
  Enraptured by their own greatness,
  Seduced by spiritual greed -
  I saw gross narcissistic devotion,
  Born out of ravenous need...

I witnessed their rampant insanity,
Smiling its sweet, sickly smile,
Sucked dry of any tinge of humanity,
It was ghastly and twisted and vile,
  I watched my husband betray me
  And saw the guru take hold,
  Of the panels at the control tower
  The mind of the group in her mould...

"This is now my family,
This is where I belong -
Mata[12] is my path and future"
Were the words of my husband's song;
       He looked awkward, soft and pathetic,
       A puppet with a broken I -
       When he looked at me it was crooked
       I knew he was saying goodbye.

I knew the battle was over,
Mata had secured her prize,
The moorings were completely broken -
There was no-one in all of their eyes;
       The Guru had landed her cunning catch,
       Distorting a message divine,
       She had lured her latest minnow
       On the bait of her fishing line.

They turned to their latest trophy
And bowed to him each in their turn,
Said one "You're a great soul Simon[13]"
What I heard was "We've got you, we've won;"
       I watched in frozen horror -
       Saw a flash of the Nazi crimes,
       I was seeing the hand of oppression
       Lived out in a sign of our times...

[12]Mata – means Mother. This was how the guru told her followers to address her.
[13]Simon was the name given to my former husband by the guru. His real name was and is Yehu.

I knew in that moment I'd witnessed
An atrocity of the soul -
And saw in a flash something epic,
A battle to do with control;
  I thought "No-one will ever believe me"
  I turned my face to the sky -
  And shuddered throughout my whole body,
  With a feeling that sliced through a cry.

The silence was violent and acrid,
I felt myself turn into stone -
The ultimate rape by "The Mindless",
By a group who had lost their way home;
  I could have lost my mind right then,
  Severed my link with mankind -
  But I sat in the midst of madness
  And prayed to have presence of mind...

This wasn't a horror movie
This wasn't a script writ in bold,
This was a living nightmare
The river of my blood had run cold;
  I talked to the soul in my husband
  And said "You know I'm your wife,
  I love you, always remember"
  And walked out to start a new life...

I'll never forget the horror,
Of grieving my husband who'd 'died' -
Knowing his mind was held hostage,
And the extent to which he had lied;
  He refused to have any contact,
  There was nothing I could do to resist -
  He just erased me from his memory
  As if I didn't exist.

I watched the man whom I'd looked up to
Disintegrate over time -
Convince himself he was carried,
By the might of the One who's sublime;
    I'd seen the man whom I'd married,
    Look at me with eyes half glazed -
    With a far-away look like a stranger
    Wandering around in a daze...

I'd seen the man whom I'd trusted
Seal the door on his mind,
Destroying all vestige of kindness
The Light had made him turn blind;
    I watched him become something *other* -
    Detached, quite thorough and cruel,
    Lost on a ladder to Heaven
    Everyone else was a fool.

"My conscience is clear, I am laughing
I am healing the sick, I'm in bliss,
You are the one who's betrayed me
You've fallen into the Abyss;
    I'm perfect and pleasant and powerful,
    I live in service to God -
    We pray for you every evening"
    - You poor little whimpering sod.

How could he do it dear Mother?
How come he became such a beast?
How come in the name of the Father
Such brutality was released?
    His arid spirituality -
    His vapid sense of self -
    His appalling superiority
    His humanity left on a shelf.

I'm obsessed with repetitive thinking,
Consumed with plotting revenge -
Overwhelmed by putrid imaginings
Exploding vile puss in my veins
       I'm owning, my innermost darkness,
       I'm touching something extreme,
       The side of my hidden nature -
       The parts I'd prefer to call dream.

Maybe the person I'm fighting,
Isn't my husband after all -
My God, I think I am seeing,
I think I'm hearing *the call;*
       Who now has lost their humanity?
       I'm reduced to a fireball of hate
       Vengeance raging inside me,
       I can neither live out, nor sate.

Where has *my loving woman* gone?
I hear a voice say "I am here"
I am sitting right beside you,
Let me hold you, and sit with your fear;
       In shock, I just keep on rocking
       Staring out blankly into space,
       I can feel a presence around me
       A golden aura of Grace...

I am held in the arm of compassion,
I let out a roar from the deep,
And think of all those in prison -
Who weren't ever able to weep;
       I could have killed my husband
       In a fit of unfettered rage,
       I think of all the murderers
       Locked up for life in a cage...

I feel my heart encompass
All those who are doing time,
　　　For acts that they've committed -
　　　Through a mindless passionate crime.

Mother! Mother! Hear us,
Help us find the way,
To forgive all those who have hurt us,
Help us find the right words to pray;
　　　Mother! Mother! Help me,
　　　Find the way to see,
　　　Not the enemy in my brother -
　　　But the one that is hidden in me...

Mother! Mother! Mend us,
Take our broken heart,
And with the balm of your infinite soothing,
Take us back to how we were at the start;
　　　Mother! Mother! Forgive us,
　　　We know not what we've done,
　　　In turning our backs on each other -
　　　We have turned away from the sun...

Mother! Mother! Heal us,
Remind us of who we are,
Of our littleness and our greatness,
How each one of us has strayed far;
　　　Mother! Mother! Show me.
　　　Give me light to see,
　　　Take my hand and guide me -
　　　Set my spirit free...

I do not know yet my destiny,
With those who cut out their heart -
But I know that in facing the enemy,
Lies the secret of the sacred healing art;
    God knows the trial of terror,
    And why in His name it is wrought,
    Just how many people have been broken
    By groups who wreak havoc through thought?

Unmask the authoritarian,
The ruler and the regime -
Liberate the controller,
Un-throttle the bottled-up scream;
    Evil's a vicious circle,
    Sins of the fathers go round -
    To be visited on their children,
    Or buried deep in the ground...

Cults will cast out their loved ones,
Wars will always be rife,
Families will shrink and shrivel -
Till we acknowledge all aspects of life;
    Until we can look in the mirror,
    And nakedly face who we are -
    And see everyone as a sinner
    And everyone as a star...

"*Mama Lizzie*" sent the unabridged version of this poem to Eric Lomax as a result of which they entered into a period of correspondence, They first met in February 2001 at an Anglo-Japanese seminar on Reconciliation in London and then again in August of the same year when Eric visited "*Mama Lizzie*" at her home in Bath. They remain in contact to this day.

BATH

The city now known as Bath was founded by the ancient Celts on the site of the only natural hot springs in England. The village was centred around the cult of Sul, goddess of the springs. When the Romans conquered England, they adopted the cult of Sul because of her similarity to their Goddess Minerva and the unusual cult of Sul-Minerva was born. They established a bath and temple complex around the springs and named the location Aquae Sulis[14] or Waters of Sul.

I moved to the World Heritage City of Bath in 1999, largely drawn by its aesthetic architectural beauty, thriving cultural life and history of healing spa waters. At the time, I was involved in promoting *Time for Peace* – an interactive arts project and believed that Bath was the perfect place to grow a peace initiative.

I initially lived in *the Circus* a stunning example of Georgian architecture by John Wood the Elder which is considered to be his masterpiece. Living in *the Circus* held great meaning and inspiration for me for a number of reasons. The name comes from the Latin 'circus' which means a ring, oval or circle and this had a resonance with the quotation by Edwin Markham and also the CANDALA® which is based on *the Circle* symbolising unity and wholeness. In addition, the circumference of *the Circus* matches, almost exactly, that of the inner circle of rocks at Stonehenge, a prehistoric monument located in the English county of Wiltshire in the South West of England and one of the most famous sites in the world. *The Circus* represents the Sun and the nearby Royal Crescent the Moon which is designed by Elder's son John Wood (the Younger).

I staged a number of community events in *the Circus* over the years: including the opening ceremony of the Bardic Festival (1999) and two candlelit peace vigils (2002 and 2003). It was in the Royal Crescent Hotel that my career as a performance poet began when I met Monireh Fritelsou, then Director of La Maison de Culture in Geneva. Monireh insisted that I wrote and perform a cabaret for Club Members in the hotel and her belief in me was so compelling that it began an extraordinary, albeit brief cycle of success, which in turn led me to Ba Kinghorn, a former thespian with the Royal Shakespeare Company who championed my work and trained me to do a one-woman show.

[14]www.aquae_sulis/index.

Bath Wrap

They say Bath is the graveyard of ambition
So I thought I'd try to prove them wrong
If I turned on the tap and wrote a Bath rap,
Would anybody pick up my song?

Is Bath more into bollards than nurturing *'Tom Stoppards'*[15]
Are we locked in a vault in the past?
Could we not inject a flavour, some of us might savour
A whiff of New York chic would be a blast!

What I'd really like to see is our whole community
With its mind heart and soul set on fire
A daily happening place full of grit, as well as grace
To liven up the dead, tired and dire.

Imagine if we could be a café society
Reminiscent of Paris in its prime,
For artists, musicians, poets, metaphysicians -
Thinkers who're ahead of their time.

We'd give birth to new ideas, shed light on foes and fears
And be real in the way that we related,
We'd not just go with the flow; we'd lead the way and boldly show
It's good to be unbound, not constipated!

Bitten by the cosmic bug, we'd give Bath a healthy plug,
As a leading spa of spirit and well-being,
A fount of inspiration for profound regeneration,
A wave of clear, blue turquoise healing.

[15]Sir Tom Stoppard OM, CBE, FRSL (born TomášS traüssler 3 July 1937) is a British
playwright, knighted in 1997. He has written prolifically for TV, radio, film and stage.

I dream of the Movers and Shakers,
  The Visionaries and Quakers,
  Gathering in service and style -
  By uniting our most gifted, Bath could be uplifted,
  If only we could go that extra mile.

I dream of this old retirement city
  With a voice both wise and witty;
  A beacon, built on pillars of the sage,
  Could we open to the new, become a forum with a view,
  A major player on the international stage?

I dream of an innovate marriage,
  A contemporary horse and carriage
  Of the Georgian and Bohemian frame of mind,
  Could we take from each the best and deftly manifest
  A spark to enlighten humankind?

I wrote *Bath Wrap* and *Chalice of the Heart* in 2002 in response to a poetry competition 'A Dream of Bath' organised by BRISLI (Bath Royal Literary & Scientific Institution) and *Bath Wrap* won first prize. Around this period, I also appeared at the Bath Literature Festival, the Mayor's Call to Prayer and at other local events. My one-woman show *Performance Piece* played at the Museum of Bath at Work in 2002 and was edited and directed by Ba. The local composer Christine Sweetman set *Chalice of the Heart* to music which was performed by Basira Ward-Davis and Simon Davis. All of the poems in this section were part of the show.

CHALICE OF THE HEART

CRESCENT OF THE MOON,
CIRCLE OF THE SUN,
BRIDGE OF HEALING HERITAGE
IN COMMUNION WITH THE ONE.

PLACE OF RENEWAL,
SPIRITUAL REBIRTH,
CONNECTION WITH THE SOURCE,
WELLSPRING OF THE EARTH.

VESSEL OF THE VALLEY,
CHALICE OF THE HEART,
HOME OF INSPIRATION,
INNOVATIVE ART.

SACRED PERFORMANCE,
EACH PART WITH ITS ROLE,
COMMUNITY REMEMBRANCE,
UNFOLDING OF THE SOUL.

CELTIC-ROMAN PATHWAY,
MYSTERY DOWN THE LINE,
HISTORY OF COMPASSION,
LIGHT THIS SPARK DIVINE.

THE GOLDEN LIGHT OF SULIS,
WARMS HER HONEY STONE,
CASTING LOVE UPON HER SHADOWS,
LIFTING SPIRITS OVERTHROWN.

THE WATERS OF MINERVA,
FLOW UPON HER SKIN,
MAY THEY PURIFY HER SOUL,
CONNECTING KITH AND KIN.

BATHE IN HER BEAUTY,
HARMONY AND GRACE,
SENSE THE PRAYERS IN THE AIR,
AS YOU ATTUNE TO HER PACE.

MAY THE ANGELS OF DREAMS,
BRING GENTLE SOFT RELEASE,
RECONCILIATION,
SPACE AND TIME FOR PEACE.

MAY BATH BE A RISEN VISION,
OF LOCAL - WORLD IMPORT,
MAY BATH BE A MILLENNIAL BEACON,
A MAGNET FOR NEW THOUGHT.

The Sulis Sister Call

What do you mean by a Sulis Sister?
    A fella asked me the other day;
It's hard to describe, but we're of one tribe -
It's about being a certain way.

You could call us a soul family,
    Together we know we belong;
It's not about formal membership -
More the fire of our inner song...

It's not what we do, our villa with a view,
    Or how many noughts we earn;
It's the light in our eyes, our desire to be wise -
What makes us live, love, ache and burn.

A Sulis Sister can be a mister,
    It's not a gender affair;
You can be single, straight, gay married or divorced -
It's about living life with energy and flair.

We come from different quarters,
    But find we're of one mind;
We're all agreed the most important thing -
Is to love and be more kind.

The Arts are like the sun to us,
    Cos they lift and move and prod;
Sometimes unexpectedly -
They provide a route to God.

Calling those who've got a vocation
    To entertain, heal, laugh and play;
Come bubble up from the wellspring -
May we blaze a new pathway!

The Sulis Sister Song

We're the sassy Sulis Sisters and we live in Bath,
We get our verve from Minerva and the healing path;
We're hot steamy women and Bath is our beat,
We're the smartest little outfit on Milsom Street.

If you savour our perfume and imbibe our vibe,
You'll get a special kind of hit that you can't describe;
You can't put it into bottles it would blow your mind,
But we give it out for free when we're feeling kind!

Have you heard the Roman city's been taken by storm,
It's in the grip of the Goddess and is under reform;
Blazers have been banned there's a movement that's new
Salsa's on the street and in the Sunday pew.

    Rhythm's the fashion
    Dance is the thing,
    Everyone's doing it to ring their ding -
    Ring ding, ring ding, ring a ding ding!

The 2010 Bath Peace Ceremony held in Parade Gardens
Organised by The Global Circle of Peace

"*Mama Lizzie*" & Margaret Gibney
lighting a Candle for Peace

Candala of Peace & Bath Abbey in the background

The original Candal of Peace © Lizzie Davies

Peace PAX Acorn & Circle
designed by Lizzie Davies & Caroline Dewison

Buccament Bay

THE CARIBBEAN

My initial introduction to the Caribbean was St. Vincent and the Grenadines and the Buccament Bay Resort where I immediately felt a soul connection with the local people and the land. The first thing I noticed on arrival was a prominent lone palm tree on top of one of the lush green hills on the riverside of the bay. This tree was, and continues to be an important source of my inspiration and meditation. Indeed, it has so etched itself in my mind and being it is perennially with me wherever I go. . .

The staff at Buccament Bay radiated great warmth, kindness and helpful service from the start and greeted my emerging writings with robust encouragement and enthusiasm. The title of my first Caribbean poem was given by a holistic therapist in the spa, Candy, who on seeing the demonstration of my new slow, laid-back swaggering walk said: "You've got *the Vincy Vibe.*" Several of the staff were particularly moved by the poem saying that they felt I had captured the 'Vincentian Spirit' and that I thought like a *Vincy!* They were also touched that I was the first person whom they new personally who had ever written about them. It was a great pleasure to reflect these beautiful, open-hearted people back to themselves and our appreciation of one another was genuine and sincere.

When it came to planning my return trip to St. Vincent, my friends asked me what I would do during my four month stay, I replied "I am going to live life and see what happens!"

I already had one or two plans as a result of a memorable, three hour meeting, with La Fayette Johnson-James, a local performance poet who also worked with an HIV support group. I had instigated the idea of *the Vincy Vibe Benefit,* and had offered my services to appear at the event in January 2012 at the Peace Memorial Hall in Kingstown. The show would help to raise funds for CARE-SVG Inc (Care Advocacy Reaching-out Empowering St. Vincent & the Grenadines) and I also wanted to explore running a course of self-empowerment for people living with HIV. Apart from this, the slate was absolutely clear for anything to happen.

I have learnt in life that not-knowing and the creation of space are vital keys in catalysing self-transformation and creativity. I believe that my willingness to return to St. Vincent in a state of deep faith, open-mindedness and receptivity allowed this book to be conceived and written, as I made myself available for the creative spirit to move through me in whatever way it wished.

The Vincy Vibe[16]

St. Vincent! Hairouna! Land of the Blessed!
For the sound of lapping wave, sway of palm -
And all the magical properties of your healing balm;
I give abundant thanks,
May the illuminating vibration of your love and calm -
Be forever protected from hurricane and harm.

"St. Vincent, I love you"
You have only to hear the lyrics of this song,
By the 'ABC' of Calypso[17],
To know this island is enchanting -
And there is a universal sense of belonging going on.

The lullaby of an eternal, maternal presence
Is hanging in the air,
Gentle, yet strong, you can hear her
Melodious sounds in the names of her children:
Nyasha, Latasha, Shanella, Orlscinda, Carlon.

Even as a newcomer,
I can feel Mother Love living on
In her sons and daughters,
In their waters, blood and skin,
"Hear my friends! Here in St. Vincent, kinship is king!"

Just eight days into my stay at Buccament Bay,
And Yes, I confess, I've got *the Vincy Vibe* -
I've imbibed the whole experience,
Savoured each exquisite morsel
And been sated by such a feast of sensual delights
In body, mind and soul,
I am high as a kite on pure, unadulterated happiness,
All those beaming smiles are contagious!

[16]Written for the spoken word.
[17]'ABC' stands for Alston Becket Cyrus, a Vincentian whose achievements and distinguished musicianship have earned him this title.

I've even got the swagger
Of the local 'walk n' talk' runnin' through me,
A laid-back bounce in my step that says
"Mmm, Me day ya 'I'm here. I'm good"

Here you cross the bridge beyond the land of sea and sand
To stand in a realm of timeless space
Imbued with grace and heartfelt hospitality
Lifting, gifting new life and harmony,
Buccament Bay is the place *to be*.

Mother Nature has cast her spell on me here
With her boundless, elemental beauty at every turn,
Scan the skyline from west to east on the riverside of the bay
Until you find a rounded hill in the form of a letter m
Way up on high stands an earthy, fronded sentinel
Proud, erect, alone.

When you see her, say a fond hello from me.
It was she who told me
"The M is for mmm the very essence of *the Vincy Vibe*
Some things you just can't describe
They're too precious to put into words."

Buccament Bay has opened the way,
For me to commune with the Vincentian Muse of Ascension;
Who needs a spliff when you can get a whiff
Of the intoxicating, flavour of creativity?

I've been given the rhythm, been set free
And am walking the highroad of serendipity
For all the magnificent blessings and caressings,
Of this beautiful people, place and land
"Mi tank you, mi luv you, "mmm, mmm, mmm!..."

Poet of the Caribbean[18]

I was swimming in the shimmering waters
Of the silky aqua sea,
When out of the blue, yet right on cue,
    A Vincy Muse whispered to me.

"Poet of the Caribbean"
That got my interest instantly,
It made me smile, and then after a while,
    I thought - Could that title belong to me?

No! Surely a knowledgeable local,
Would have more a vocal right to the post,
Writing about life on the islands,
    Performing from coast to coast.

Nevertheless, I thought I'd undress,
And try on the mantle for size,
If an authentic fit, and I were 'it',
    A natural wit would open my eyes.

So I set sail with my imagination,
The constellation as my constant guide,
Inspiration as my trusted companion,
    And wondered what new vista would open wide.

[18]Written for the spoken word.

A poet is at home on the ocean,
And in the universal world of the deep,
Inspired by waves of emotion,
    Wizardry of words is the crop that we reap.

When a *Poet of the Caribbean*,
Is drunk on rum from the sky,
Words manifest from the boundless treasure chest,
    And come tumbling in from way on high.

Could a pyrotechnic poet be a match,
For a pirate with a patch?
It is an unlikely mix, but a Muse could fix it,
    Any fish can be their catch!

Even that rogue and famous character
Depicted by the actor you-know–who
The one who shoots an arrow right through your heart
    And shot the film in the bay at Wallilabou[19].

What a perfect location that set would make
A great vision for the Grenadines
Of a *Vincy Vibe* artists' colony
    Where performance poets are kings and queens.

---

[19]The main Caribbean location for all the "Pirates of the Caribbean" movies. The films starred Johnny Depp as Jack Sparrow.

Imagine a centre of creativity,
Where the spoken word flies like a bird,
On the wings of unseen helpers,
    Giving voice to lives yet unheard.

Picture *Poets of the Caribbean*,
Regaling people with stories of gold,
Of living history, spiced with mystery,
    Passing on ancestral lines manifold.

Visitors like me to St. Vincent,
Would be enraptured by their colourful tales,
It could open up new horizons,
    And put a whole new wind in their sails.

Poet of the Caribbean,
I feel a new appointment coming on,
A job with heart born of genuine art,
    Delivered with panache and aplomb!

Blue Moon[20]

The cool blue moon smiled upon me
On a quiet, wide, open day;
All was still as I pondered the hill
And my tree on Buccament Bay.

Rejoicing in the emerald lushness
And the bounty of Mother Earth;
My heart went out to greet her
To give thanks for my rebirth.

At one with sun and water
Gentle breeze and moving sky;
I sat outside of time and dwelt
In the land where miracles lie.

Returning to this mortal plane
I went upon my way;
Feeling in the flow, where would I go
Now my instrument was at play?

Then an old familiar discourse
Started running through my head;
Which part of myself would win the day
To be watered, fed and led?

As I meandered across the piazza
I couldn't help but notice that my gait,
Wasn't leading me straight to my villa
But to the café where temptation lay in wait!

Seduced by the ice cream parlour
With my chocolate fever running high,
I eyed the troughs of frozen delights
And succumbed with a sensual sigh.

[20]Written for the spoken word.

Full of the joys of bonhomie
I turned to the man in the queue,
And seeing the crowd around him said -
"I see you've brought your tribe along with you."

We struck up a conversation,
He introduced me to his family,
Then with cone in hand, I left his band
And withdrew to let them simply be.

To my surprise the man came over,
Sat down and then enquired,
"What brought you here?" With an air sincere,
I responded with a line that was inspired.

'The spirit is the shortest answer",
It was the simplest explanation I could give,
Yet I wondered what he would make of it,
And if our conversation would continue to live.

I told him about the forthcoming Benefit,
That I was putting out the call,
And would love to invite his family
To the gig at Peace Memorial Hall.

I shared my heart was in the arts,
I was in St. Vincent on vacation,
Had started to do some voluntary work,
And planned to meet the Minister of Education.

He said "Be sure to tell her
The Prime Minister is far from fine,
He's totally devoid of culture
He's a complete hick and philistine."

Doubting myself for a moment,
Putting what I'd been told on a shelf,
I said, 'That's strange that's not what I've heard.
But if true, I'll just have to educate him myself!"

"Do you know who I am?" he twinkled,
I said "I've no idea, but from what I read
I think you are a big man, yet simple,
A man of the earth in word and deed."

Enter stage left, my friend Gennine
Bursting with excitement and energy,
"I told you, you should meet him Lizzie,
Now you see - it's happened naturally."

I was lost and deeply puzzled,
My brain did a double-take,
I was missing a piece of the jigsaw,
Something invisible was clearly at stake.

She got it! "You've no idea who you're talking to?"
I said "I haven't a clue,
Please tell me what is going on?"
I'd begun to feel in a stew.

Then I froze in a fractured moment
In the aeons of a pregnant pause,
Whilst I furiously scanned my inner library
For information to open new doors.

Then everything stopped, the penny dropped,
The man extended his hand;
"Hello, I'm Ralph Gonsalves
The Prime Minister of the land."

Soul Goal[21]

I was a total football virgin
When I set foot on Vincentian shores;
But soon I was inducted,
    Into its rules and local lores.

It was Susan, wife of Colwyn the Coach,
Of the national team Vincy Heat -
Who said "You must write a poem about them, for your book,
    It'll make it more authentic and complete."

So off I went to ponder...
And kicked a few ideas around,
To see if this soul could score a home goal
    And lift a poem with an angle off the ground.

My foray into football
Was an enlightening education;
It ended up with no World Cup
    But a feat of memorisation.

To further the cause I attended a match
At the stadium Arnos Vale,
Which was great, but I'd left my specs at home
    Which was a sure sign something would prevail...

Fresh to the game and all fired up,
I strained to see the numbers etched in black;
On the green shirts of my adopted team -
    Then heard "It's the yellow shirts Lizzie, Welcome back!"

Undeterred, with sight still blurred,
I followed the ball as best I could -
With Susan giving a running commentary
    On strategy and lingo which was good!

[21]Written for the spoken word.

Next I heard the players all had *play-names,*
I had to wrap my head around that one;
To see how I could recognise who was who,
What was what and what they'd done.

There was Shrek real name Reginald,
With arms akimbo standing bold;
And Left Eye, real name, Myron
With luminous shoes lemony gold.

As you can see my powers of observation,
By this time were simple like a child;
With all the visual and auditory stimuli
My brain was fried and over-filed.

By the time they blew the whistle,
And I met the members of Vincy Heat;
I confess I was really struggling
To keep the whole thing moving and upbeat.

There was Acer meaning Rasta,
Real name Victor, the kit man with a cap;
And Tall Man real name Dwayne,
Who wrote motivational words and rap.

There was Manage real name Theon,
With a handshake firm and strong;
And then I really lost it,
The list of names was just too long...

Nevertheless I promised to do my best,
To see if I could write
Something that would rally their spirits,
And cause the blood in their veins to fight.

How could we stand with the brothers of the band,
United in a way that would serve?
Vincy Heat *and* St. Vincent
So a new pride would be their preserve?

There must be a way to make the nation play
As a whole and get the fans on side;
So that losing the game didn't incite blame,
    Or split the nation in two - the big divide...

Rising to the challenge,
Not one to say I can't,
"*Mama Lizzie*" was on a mission,
    To write a simple, catchy football chant.

I consulted with those who were in the know,
Researched the popular ones on offer;
Undaunted I put on my thinking cap,
    To see what I could proffer.

Get the goal in your body and soul Vincy Heat,
Get the goal; get the Vincy Vibe beat,
Get the goal in your body and soul Vincy Heat
    Get the goal, get the Vincy Vibe beat.

Who better than Fireman Hooper
To set it to a Soca rhythm beat
This master of hype and entertainment
    Would get the crowd up and moving on its feet!

If all goes well and time will tell,
We'll sing the chant at Peace Memorial Hall;
And invite the whole of the audience -
    To unite behind our team – one and all...

It's up to the role of team spirit,
To help Vincy Heat raise their game;
And inspire the voice of the nation -
    To support them whilst they rise to fame.

Fingers crossed this spark will take,
Fans and mascots will take up the cause;
To fan the flames of their national team,
    And put fire in their belly with applause.

Rich Material[22]

"When I bought my first Rolex ..."

Sky Channel

I'd rather watch the sky than the television,
A voice pronounced itself to me;
At the end of watching a sunset for hours,
And the moon light the dark, inky sea.

With the sound of the crickets in the foreground -
And the rhythmic waves in my being;
I was at one with the essence of simplicity,
Nature's way is infinitely freeing.

[22]Found Poem.

"Mama Lizzie"

A sudden wave of yearning moved through her
In a passionate, emotional release;
It came from the dark, deep fathoms in a flash
And was gone in a wake of silent peace...

Her burning eyes locked still with mine,
Her tiny statement was vast and bold;
In eight simple words,
Her thirty nine years were told.

"I'm going to adopt you as my mother"
It was all that needed to be said,
Then next day, came the blessing of the naming,
She was inspired to bestow upon my head.

"I'm going to call you "Mama Lizzie","
It was a moment that was sweet and profound,
As if a hidden hand had planned it all,
And through God's love, together we'd been bound.

What she didn't know, was that two years ago,
Bereft of my blood family,
I had prayed to be adopted,
And be given children in my life by God's decree.

My Sister My Sister

Isn't it wonderful how words can cross boundaries,
Of race and place and time,
Providing common ground
Through their rhythm and sound,
Through their depth and spirit and rhyme.

"My sister, my sister,
I want to learn to be the poem like you,
I'm your No.1 fan"
This poetic young man,
Is a rapper with a future in my view!

Three Early Birds

An aged morning ritual
In the quiet gentle light,
A sisterly devotional
As the sun grew ever bright.

Three early birds
Bobbing heads above the sea,
Silver dreads, shower cap
Close crop - this trinity.

Linking hands a voice rang out
In praise and exultation,
Although apart, I felt my heart
Rejoice in their meditation.

Citizen of Heaven

I knocked on the door of the indigo sky,
Would it open up and speak to me
To reveal how I could travel home
To the bosom of my family?

The guidance was unequivocal,
The stars had heard my plea;
Keep your eyes upon the heavens -
Enter the world of eternity.

Be bonded not by blood but by spirit,
Be reminded of your destiny;
The ladder of life is yours to climb -
Embody the celestial mystery.

That night I had a dream about mirrors,
The reflections that we choose to see;
How our pictures can be distorted -
By our view of reality.

What if grief, pain and suffering,
Were not seen as a punishment from hell;
But the carving out of a deep inner hole -
To be filled as a living well?

An absence on the earthly plane,
In whatever form that may be;
When seen with new eyes can be a presence
Of a spiritual reality.

Is our choice then to pray to have vision?
To ponder what we need to hear;
To raise our gaze to the heavens,
And be at one with the Healer and the Seer?

THE QUEST

To tread the path of self-knowledge is a life-long quest and a universal journey of the soul. Many things can offer portals of self-discovery along the way. I offer these four poems which come from different stages of my quest. Each one focuses on a key subject and jointly they form the cornerstone of this book. Together I feel they tell the story of my journey and I hope that they and the rest of this book, will serve you on yours.

Mirror Mirror

Mirror mirror on the wall,
Who's the scariest of them all?
Hidden from view without reflection,
The *other one* – your own projection.

Error, error in the mind,
Lift the veil on the one who's blind,
Answer, answer in your cave,
Reveal your dark secret - prior to your grave.

Embracing the Enemy

Fear's a funny thing you know,
It can make us shrink *and* grow;
It's a paradox rather like life,
We can choose to ignore it -
Or discover we have stored it
And deal with our inner strife.

It's only when we face
And embrace our fear
That our enemy becomes our *friend*,
Which you could say
Is the essence of my story,
As I hope it might be yours - before your end?

Be Original - Be Yourself

Poetry's a pathway to commune -
A way to stay in tune
And wire up the dots of our brain,
Let's put love in our connections -
Light in our reflections,
And make our world a little more sane.

The beat and rhythm in our bod
Is a strong divining rod,
So we can plug straight into the mains -
By reaching up on high
From the earth to the sky;
Inspiration can flood our inner planes.

In tapping the Divine
And the bards down the line;
We are reviving the language of the soul,
In reaching out to be heard
Through the power of the word;
We are reminded of our spiritual role.

Knowing the dark of night,
Becoming an instrument of light;
Isn't this what life is all about?
Coming through adversity,
Can be our university -
Be original - Be yourself;
Dare to come out!

Mellower Than Ever

I travelled down a long, long, lane
That took me deep inside;
From the pell-mell of my busy mind
To somewhere still and wide.

Cocooned by calm and confidence -
The air was clear and bright;
I could see far all around me,
And felt a dawning light.

Mellower than ever
Meditating on release;
I smiled and got the message
And was filled with inner peace.

Someone was gently calling -
I could barely hear their voice;
Till a wind blew soft the clouds apart,
And offered me a choice.

Which one of you is it going to be?
Who rules your inner state?
Is it war or peace you want to make?
To destroy or to create?

Mellower than ever
Meditating on release,
    I smiled and got the message -
    And was filled with inner peace...

In tasting Nature's nectar,
Our mood can be controlled,
    By a life-enhancing drug that's free -
    And worth far more than gold.

Peace of mind is here and now -
If only we can see,
    The present is for everyone,
    To be, or not to be?

SHARING THE PEACE

It is widely recognised that everything in life comes round full circle.

The next three pieces are a part of Peace PAX[23].

My Universal Dream

I wrote the poem *My Universal Dream* in 2009 to encapsulate and share the essence of my vision for personal and world peace and to offer it as an opportunity for the people of the world to come together in the creation of a communal peace offering. It correlates to the Einstein quote and understanding which underpin the creation of Peace PAX.

"You cannot solve a problem from the same level of consciousness that created it. You must learn to see the world anew."

Join with me, and a growing body of people, in imagining the global community uniting in this simple yet profound and effective act of peace.

Time for Peace on Earth

Time for Peace on Earth is a choreographed mime-poem and meditation which was inspired by the idea of tying a turquoise ribbon on a tree as a universal peace offering. It was created a few weeks before the first *Time for Peace* tree-planting ceremony at Prinknash Abbey in Gloucestershire on 14th March 1998 and was performed for the first time on that occasion. Abbot Francis encouraged Lizzie to take the work into schools and the piece was added to the body of creative work that *Time for Peace* promoted at that time.

"*Mama Lizzie*" and Margaret Gibney, Leading Light and Director of The Global Circle of Peace and former Young Ambassador for UNICEF, recorded a teaching video in August 2011 which you can view on *YouTube*[24].

---

[23]A Resource Pack of interactive, multimedia material to cultivate inner and outer peace, www.theglobalcircleofpeace.com/peace-pax.
[24]www.youtube.com/watch?v=eXUDbvGelWg.

The Circle of Peace Dedication

The Circle of Peace Dedication[25] has a core message and invites people around the world to use their creativity to share it with others through song. It is based on the four lines of the second verse of *Time for Peace on Earth*.

My Universal Dream

I have a dream, a wonderful plan,
For every child, woman and man
To light a candle and be still,
As a gift of peace and world goodwill.

Time to be silent, time to be,
Time to rest in eternity;
At any time of night or day,
Be at one, for this I pray.

[25]Compose and record your own original version or use the sheet music online go to www.theglobalcircleofpeace.com/get-involved/

Time for Peace on Earth

Tie a turquoise ribbon
On every single tree,
Say a little prayer for peace
For our world for you and me.

Peace in every home and heart,
Peace across our land,
Peace in every mind and body,
Peace in every hand.

Peace on all our children,
And every living thing,
Peace on the road to forgiveness,
That the angels always bring...

Peace in every village,
Peace in every town,
Peace in every single city,
Peace on every crown.

Peace in every nation,
Peace in every race,
Peace in every word and deed,
Peace on every face.

Peace in our awakening,
Peace in our rebirth,
Time for peace for everyone,
Time for peace on earth.

The Circle of Peace Dedication

Peace in every home and heart,
Peace across our land,
Peace in every mind and body,
Peace in every hand.

Author's Note

St. Vincent and the Grenadines has been a supremely healing and peaceful place in which to conceive and write 'Poet of the Caribbean.' I am deeply grateful for having had this opportunity and owe much to the beauty and energy of the natural environment here, which has allowed inspiration to flow. It seems entirely fitting that I should draw this work to a close in my beloved hills above Buccament Bay where I have been staying with a local family and where I have written the majority of this book.

I can think of no better way to end my *musings as a global peacemaker* than to extend a warm personal invitation to you, your family, friends and community, to do all that you possibly can to help spread the word about Peace PAX.

Together, we can help to realise a universal vision of Creativity, Unity and Peace in our world.

St. Vincent and the Grenadines
November 2011

WEBSITES OF INTEREST

theglobalcircleofpeace.com
peaceoneday.org
justonedaybooks.com
buildingbridgesforpeace.org
peacedirect.co.uk

* * *

nonviolentcommunication.com
temenosacademy.org

* * *

jungclub.london.org
transpersonalcentre.co.uk
psychosynthesis.edu

* * *

martinpowellpoetryblogspot.com
mamalizzie.com

CPSIA information can be obtained at www.ICGtesting.com
Printed in the USA
BVOW011556080713

325352BV00011B/451/P